EDGE
BOOKS™

# HOW TO DRAW
# DRAGONS, TROLLS,
## AND OTHER DANGEROUS MONSTERS

BY A.J. SAUTTER
Featuring 5 Artists

CAPSTONE PRESS
a capstone imprint

Edge Books are published by Capstone Press,
1710 Roe Crest Drive, North Mankato, Minnesota 56003
www.mycapstone.com

**Library of Congress Cataloging-in-Publication Data**
Sautter, Aaron, author.
How to draw dragons, trolls, and other dangerous monsters / by A.J. Sautter.
 pages cm.—(Edge books. Drawing fantasy creatures)
Includes bibliographical references.
Summary: "Simple, step-by-step instructions teach readers how to draw dragons, trolls,
and several other dangerous fantasy monsters"—Provided by publisher.
ISBN 978-1-4914-8023-6 (library binding)
ISBN 978-1-4914-8407-4 (eBook PDF)
1. Dragons in art—Juvenile literature. 2. Monsters in art—Juvenile literature. 3. Drawing—
Technique—Juvenile literature. I. Title.
NC825.D72S38 2016
743'.87—dc23
                                                    2015026126

**Editorial Credits**
Kyle Grenz, designer; Kelly Garvin, media researcher; Gene Bentdahl, production specialist

**Illustration Credits**
Capstone Press: Colin Howard, cover, 1, 10-11, 12-13, Jason Juta, cover, back cover, 1, 8-9,
16-17, 24-25, 26-27, Martin Bustamante, cover, 1, 14-15, 18-19, Stefano Azzalin, 20-21, 22-23,
Tom McGrath, cover, 1, 6-7, 28-31

**Design Elements**
Capstone Press; Shutterstock: aopsan, Bambuh, blue pencil, Kompaniets, Marta Jonina,
Molodec, val lawless

Printed in the United States of America, in North Mankato Minnesota.
092015    009221CGS16

# TABLE OF CONTENTS

# DRAWING DANGEROUS MONSTERS

Fantasy worlds are often overflowing with deadly monsters waiting to attack their next victim. Giants, trolls, and ogres like to ambush unwitting travelers in the mountains. Meanwhile, dragons enjoy attacking cities and strongholds to add to their treasure.

These dangerous monsters and others don't really exist, but they often thrive in our imaginations. Do you like to draw your own fantastic creatures and fantasy worlds? If so, then this book is for you! Grab some paper and pencils and prepare to set your imagination free. First follow the drawing steps to begin sketching dragons, trolls, giants, and other dangerous monsters. After practicing them, you can try drawing them in different settings or situations. You can even create scenes showing your favorite monsters battling each other. Then when your art is ready, you can color it using colored pencils, markers, or paint. Get ready to set your inner artist free!

# FINDING YOUR STYLE

Don't worry if your drawings aren't exactly like those you see in this book. Every artist has his or her own style. If you keep practicing, your own art style will develop over time. Soon you'll be creating awesome creatures and fantasy artwork of your very own.

# GATHER YOUR SUPPLIES

Before you can start drawing, you'll need to gather some basic supplies. With the following materials in hand, you'll be ready to sketch anything your imagination can create.

black marker pens

unlined paper

erasers

pencil sharpener

colored pencils or markers

sharp pencils

5

# RED DRAGONS

Red dragons have terrible tempers. They'll attack anyone who intrudes on their territories. Red dragons are also extremely greedy. They guard their huge treasure hoards fiercely. If even a single coin is stolen, they'll fly into a terrible rage and burn nearby farms and villages to the ground to find the thief.

**SIZE**: 150 FEET (46 METERS) LONG OR MORE; WINGSPANS UP TO 180 FEET (55 M)

**HABITAT**: LAIRS IN DEEP CAVES FOUND IN THE LARGEST MOUNTAIN RANGES

**Physical Features:** When these dragons hatch from their eggs, they're a bright shade of red. Their scales become dark red or red-gold as they age. Red dragons have razor-sharp claws and teeth, and powerful whiplike tails. Of course, red dragons are most famous for their fiery breath that is hot enough to melt steel.

**1**

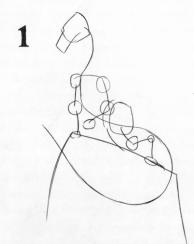

**2**

**3**

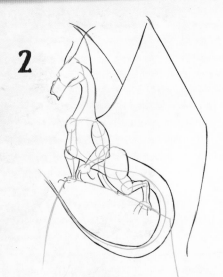

**4**

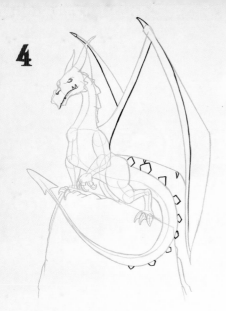

## WHAT'S NEXT?

After practicing this dragon, try to draw it attacking a mountain village. Show it flying over and blasting the buildings with its fiery breath.

# FINAL

**5**

**6**

# WHITE DRAGONS

White dragons aren't as ferocious as red dragons or as cruel as black dragons. But they do have long memories. They've been known to seek revenge against those who insulted them many years before. Like most dragons, white dragons love treasure. But they especially enjoy glittering diamonds and silver coins.

**SIZE:** ABOUT 100 FEET (31 M) LONG; WINGSPANS UP TO 120 FEET (37 M)

**HABITAT:** LAIRS IN ICY CAVES FOUND ON MOUNTAIN PEAKS OR LARGE ICEBERGS

**Physical Features:** Young white dragons are very light in color. As they age their scales darken slightly or turn light blue. Unlike other dragons, white dragons have only two legs. But they do have wickedly sharp claws and teeth. White dragons also have an icy breath weapon that can freeze their enemies solid in an instant.

**1**

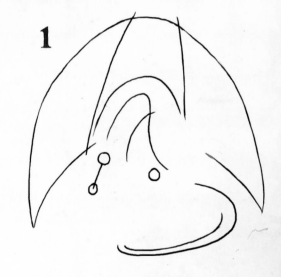

**2**

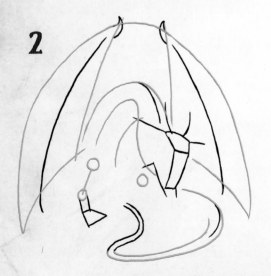

**3**

## WHAT'S NEXT?

Next draw another white dragon hunting for its next meal. Show it using its icy breath to freeze its prey.

**FINAL**

**4**

**5**

9

# BLACK DRAGONS

Black dragons are cruel and evil. They are known to enjoy hunting and killing other creatures simply to cause pain and suffering. Black dragons also love to hoard treasure. They tend to like gold coins more than gems or other valuable items.

**SIZE**: UP TO 120 FEET (37 M) LONG; WINGSPANS UP TO 150 FEET (46 M)

**HABITAT**: LAIRS IN HIDDEN CAVES OFTEN FOUND IN SWAMPS OR DARK JUNGLES

**Physical Features:** Most black dragons have thin, bony bodies. Their skin often appears diseased. The thin skin on their wings tends to tear easily, so most don't fly well. Like most dragons, black dragons have deadly claws, teeth, and tails. Their hot acid breath weapon is strong enough to dissolve even the thickest of armor.

**3**

**1**

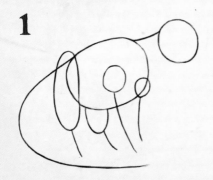

**2**

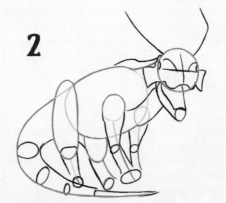

**5**

**4**

**6**

**FINAL**

## WHAT'S NEXT?

Next try to draw this dragon inside its swampy lair as it guards its huge treasure of gold coins.

# EASTERN DRAGONS

Eastern dragons are known for being wise and helpful toward humans. Eastern dragons are sometimes said to magically bring rain to help farmers' crops grow during a drought. Eastern dragons are not greedy for treasure like other dragons. But they do like colorful gems such as rubies and emeralds.

**SIZE:** MORE THAN 200 FEET (61 M) LONG
**HABITAT:** LAIRS IN HIDDEN CAVES NEAR RIVERS AND LAKES

**Physical Features:** Eastern dragons are usually brightly colored. They have camel-like heads, giant snakelike bodies, and eaglelike talons on their feet. Eastern dragons do not have a breath weapon. They also don't have wings. But they do have a magical ability to fly.

**1**

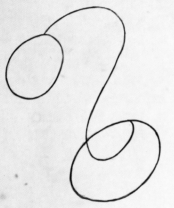

**2**

**3**

**4**

**5**

**6**

# FINAL

## WHAT'S NEXT?

After practicing the Eastern dragon, try drawing a scene showing it flying with a young person riding on its back.

# MOUNTAIN GIANTS

Mountain giants like to live alone and can be dangerous when disturbed by outsiders. They often use huge, spiked clubs to smash enemies to the ground. Mountain giants sometimes engage in mock battles by hurling giant boulders at each other. After these battles, mountain valleys often look as if a large landslide has taken place.

**SIZE**: 45 FEET (14 M) TALL OR MORE
**HABITAT**: LARGE CAVES IN MOUNTAIN RANGES; SOME LARGE HOMES IN HIDDEN VALLEYS

**Physical Features:** Other than their enormous size, mountain giants look similar to humans. But their skin is thick and tough, and it is often a stonelike gray color. Mountain giants usually have black, brown, or fiery red hair. Most males also grow huge, bushy beards.

**1**

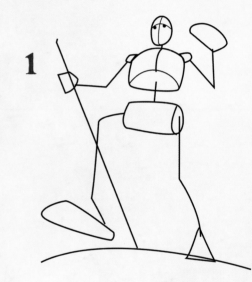

**2**

**3**

**4**

## WHAT'S NEXT?

After drawing this huge giant, try drawing two of them throwing huge boulders at each other across a mountain valley.

## FINAL

**5**

# CYCLOPES

Cyclopes usually live alone and spend their days tending to their herds of animals. Many Cyclopes are also clever blacksmiths. They make high-quality weapons and armor. It's thought that some Cyclopes have created powerful magical items in their secret forges deep inside volcanoes.

**SIZE**: ABOUT 15 FEET (4.6 M) TALL

**HABITAT**: MOUNTAIN CAVES OR THE RUINS OF OLD STONE CASTLES

**Physical Features:** Cyclopes have stocky bodies and large, strong hands. They have tough skin that is often green or a stony gray color. Most Cyclopes don't have much hair, but a few may have thin beards. Cyclopes are best known for the single large eyes in the middle of their foreheads.

**1**

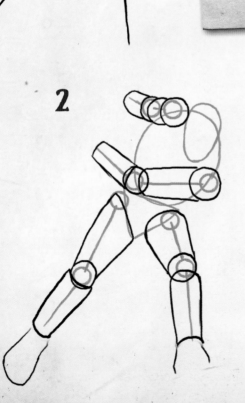

**2**

**3**

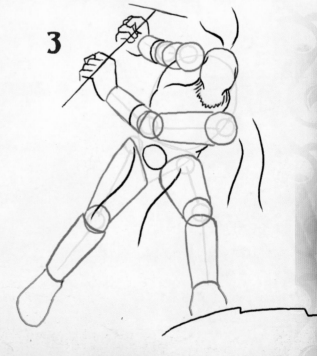

**4**

**5**

## WHAT'S NEXT?

Next draw a Cyclops forging a magical sword or shield. Try to show it working in its secret underground workshop.

**FINAL**

# ETTINS

Ettins normally live alone in dark caves that stink of decaying food. They never bathe and are usually covered in layers of smelly dirt and grime. In spite of their multiple heads, ettins aren't very intelligent. However, they are skilled with multiple weapons in combat. Ettins are fierce fighters and will usually fight to the death.

**SIZE**: ABOUT 20 TO 25 FEET (6 TO 7.6 M) TALL

**HABITAT**: DARK UNDERGROUND CAVES IN REMOTE ROCKY REGIONS

**Physical Features:** Ettins have tall, muscular bodies with two or more heads. Each head controls a different part of the body. Their thick skin is tough and protects them as a natural form of armor. Their hair is often long and stringy and is usually black or dark brown. Some ettins may also grow thick, bushy beards.

**2**

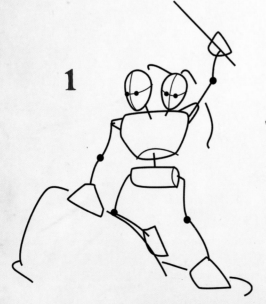

**1**

## WHAT'S NEXT?

When you're finished drawing this ettin, try drawing him again as he battles against a nasty ogre or troll.

3

4

FINAL

5

19

# OGRES

Ogres are naturally violent and cruel. They enjoy torturing enemies and love hearing them cry out in pain. Ogres aren't very intelligent and have few skills. They often go on night raids to steal food and other goods that they can't make themselves. Although sunlight doesn't harm ogres, they hate it and avoid it whenever possible.

**SIZE**: 8 TO 10 FEET (2.4 TO 3 M) TALL

**HABITAT**: DARK, DAMP CAVES IN FOOTHILLS NEAR MOUNTAINS; SOME LIVE NEAR STINKING BOGS OR SWAMPS

**Physical Features:** Ogres have incredibly strong and muscular bodies. They also have very tough skin, which is usually green or gray-green in color. Ogres also often have shortened legs, hunched backs, and other deformities. Many ogres have sharp tusks growing from their bottom jaws.

**1**

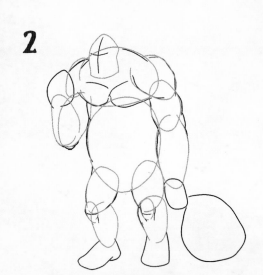

**2**

**3**

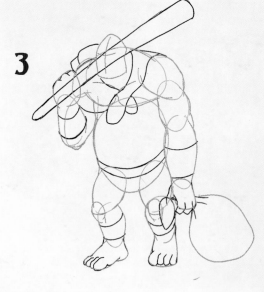

**5**

**6**

**4**

# FINAL

## WHAT'S NEXT?

Now try to draw a small group of ogres going on a nighttime raid at a local village. Show each ogre carrying a different kind of weapon to use in a fight.

# CAVE TROLLS

Cave trolls are active only at night. If they're exposed to direct sunlight, their bodies turn to solid stone. Cave trolls spend most of their time looking for food and will often steal animals from nearby farms. Some cave trolls live with groups of orcs in the mountains. They'll fight alongside the orcs to ambush unsuspecting travelers in exchange for food.

**SIZE**: 10 TO 12 FEET (3 TO 3.7 M) TALL
**HABITAT**: DEEP, DARK CAVES IN HILLS AND MOUNTAIN REGIONS

**Physical Features:** Cave trolls are related to giants, which helps explain their huge size and strength. Cave trolls' tough skin strongly resembles rough stone. These dangerous creatures also have mouths filled with sharp jagged teeth and two large tusks.

**1**

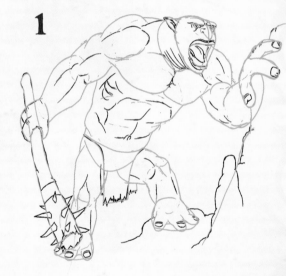

**2**

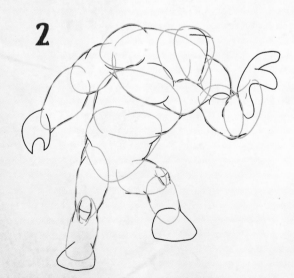

**3**

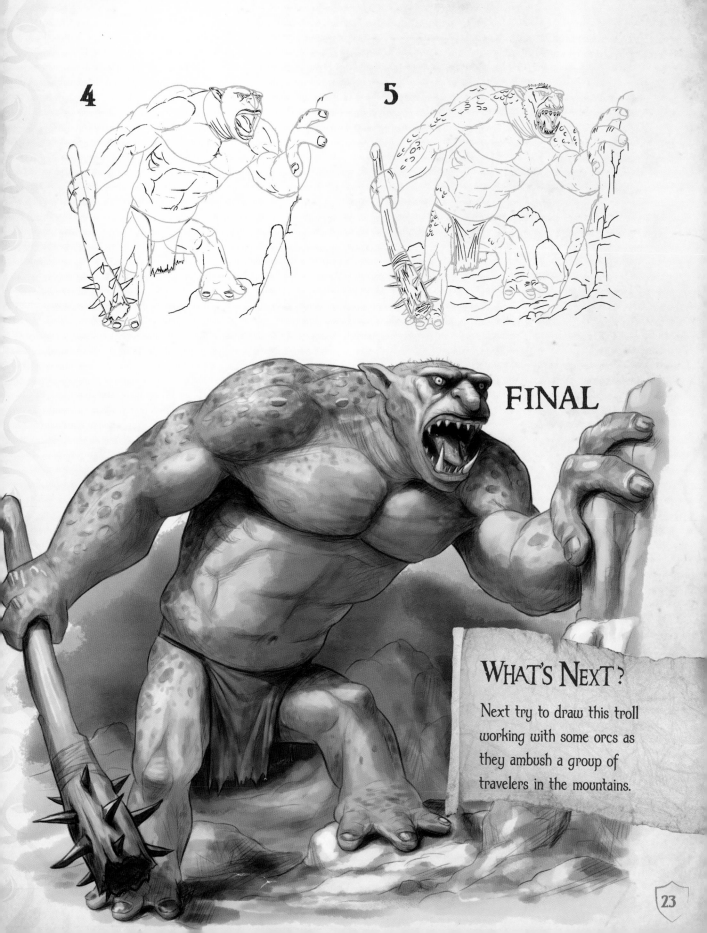

**4**

**5**

FINAL

## WHAT'S NEXT?

Next try to draw this troll
working with some orcs as
they ambush a group of
travelers in the mountains.

# FOREST TROLLS

Forest trolls have rarely been seen. It's thought that they spend most of their time roaming the forest looking for food. A few forest trolls may wear armor and carry simple weapons. These trolls are known to attack intruders and will track down enemies through the thickest forests.

**1**

**SIZE**: 12 TO 15 FEET (3.7 TO 4.6 M) TALL
**HABITAT**: DARK CAVES FOUND IN THICK FORESTS IN NORTHERN REGIONS

**Physical Features:** Forest trolls are strong and muscular with long arms and short legs. They usually have gray or green-gray skin. But many are covered in coarse brown hair. Forest trolls have huge mouths filled with jagged, rotten teeth. They also have large tusks jutting out from their lower jaws.

**2**

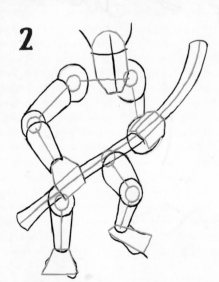

**3**

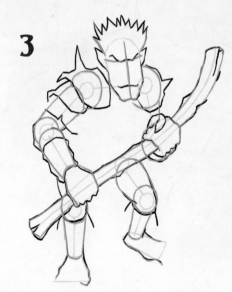

**4**

**5**

**FINAL**

## WHAT'S NEXT?

After drawing this troll, try drawing it chasing some dwarves through the thick forest.

# SWAMP TROLLS

Swamp trolls are little more than savage beasts. They aren't intelligent, can't speak, and are very violent. They usually attack all living creatures on sight. Luckily, swamp trolls are sensitive to sunlight. They normally stay in their lairs during the day and are active only at night.

**SIZE**: 8 TO 10 FEET (2.4 TO 3 M) TALL
**HABITAT**: SWAMPS AND BOGS IN TROPICAL REGIONS

**Physical Features:** Swamp trolls aren't as large as other trolls, but they're incredibly strong. Their skin is usually dark green or black in color. Swamp trolls have strong hands tipped with wicked claws they use to slash at their prey. Swamp trolls heal quickly from wounds. They can also regrow lost arms or legs within minutes. Fire and acid are the only things that can destroy them.

**1**

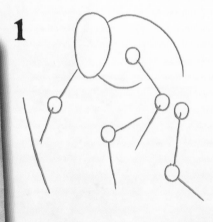

**2**

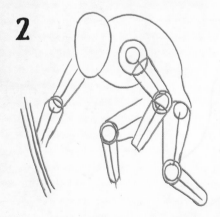

**3**

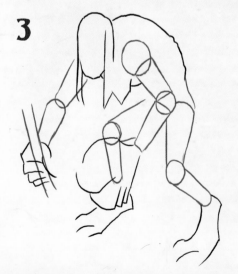

**4**

**5**

## FINAL

### WHAT'S NEXT?

Now try to draw a scene of another two swamp trolls fighting each other in a stinking swamp.

# DRAGON VS. KNIGHT

Fantasy stories are filled with tales of brave knights battling huge, fire-breathing dragons. These armored warriors test their courage by attempting a deadly task that most people wouldn't dare to try. Many of these bold knights come to a fiery end in their quest. But those who succeed often find fame, fortune, and glory. Their daring deeds live forever in stories and songs.

## DRAGON

**SIZE**: 150 FEET (46 METERS) LONG OR MORE; WINGSPANS UP TO 180 FEET (55 M)

**HABITAT**: DEEP CAVES FOUND IN THE LARGEST MOUNTAIN RANGES

## KNIGHT

**SIZE**: 6 TO 6.5 FEET (1.8 TO 2 M) TALL

**HOMES**: STRONG CASTLES OR FORTRESSES MADE OF STONE

**1**

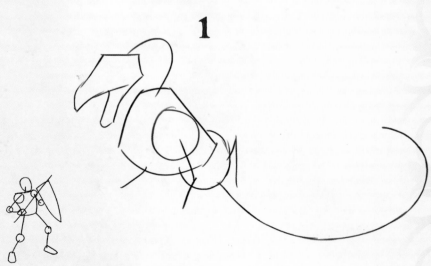

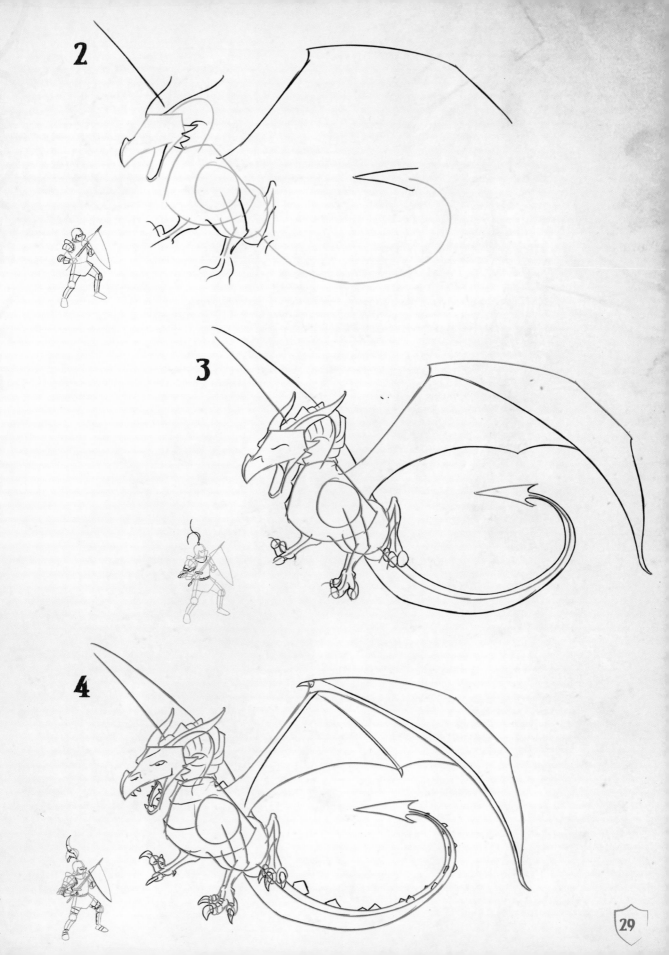

2

3

4

5

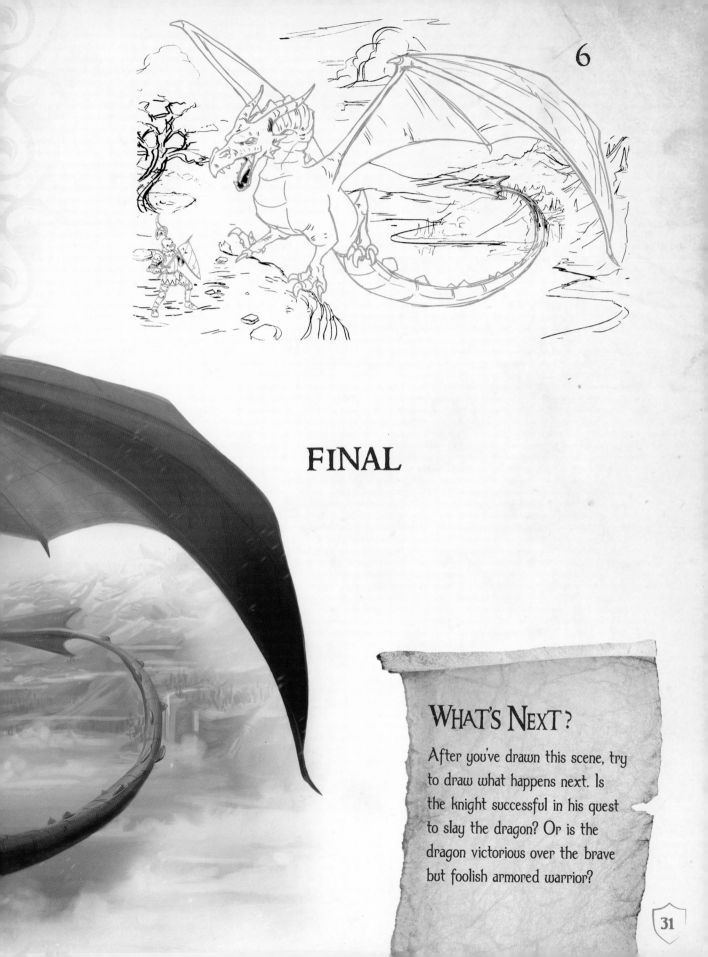

6

# FINAL

## WHAT'S NEXT?

After you've drawn this scene, try to draw what happens next. Is the knight successful in his quest to slay the dragon? Or is the dragon victorious over the brave but foolish armored warrior?

# READ MORE

**Berry, Bob.** *How to Draw Magical, Monstrous & Mythological Creatures.* Irvine, Calif.: Walter Foster Publishing, 2012.

**Nash, Mike, (et al.)** *How to Draw the Meanest, Most Terrifying Monsters.* Drawing, North Mankato, Minn.: Capstone Press, 2012.

**O'Connor, William.** *Dracopedia, the Great Dragons: An Artist's Field Guide and Drawing Journal.* Cincinnati, Ohio: IMPACT Books, 2012.

# INTERNET SITES

FactHound offers a safe, fun way to find Internet sites related to this book. All of the sites on FactHound have been researched by our staff.

Here's all you do:

Visit *www.facthound.com*

Type in this code: 9781491480236

 **Super-cool stuff!** Check out projects, games and lots more at **www.capstonekids.com**